Klingon Next Door: Off Duty the Warrior's Way
ISBN: 9781835412916

Published by
Titan Books
A division of Titan Publishing Group Ltd
144 Southwark St
London
SE1 0UP

www.titanbooks.com

First edition:
2 4 6 8 10 9 7 5 3 1

EU RP (for authorities only)
eucomply OÜ Pärnu mnt 139b-14 11317
Talinn, Estonia
hello@eucompliancepartner.com
+3375690241

TM & © 2025 CBS Studios Inc. © 2025 Paramount Pictures Corp. *Star Trek*
and related marks and logos are trademarks of CBS Studios Inc.
All Rights Reserved.

Did you enjoy this book? We love to hear from our readers.
Please e-mail us at: readerfeedback@titanemail.com or write to
Reader Feedback at the above address.

To receive advance information, news, competitions, and exclusive offers
online, please sign up for the Titan newsletter on our website:
www.titanbooks.com

No part of this publication may be reproduced, stored in a retrieval system,
or transmitted, in any form or by any means without the prior written
permission of the publisher, nor be otherwise circulated in any form of
binding or cover other than that in which it is published and without a similar
condition being imposed on the subsequent purchaser.

A CIP catalogue record for this title is available from the British Library.

Printed in China.

STAR TREK
KLINGON NEXT DOOR
OFF DUTY THE WARRIOR'S WAY

New York Times Bestseller
JOEY SPIOTTO

Tıtan BOOKS

Introduction

"Who's the best captain?" is a debate that has raged through the *Star Trek* fandom for decades. It has never been settled and can never be solved. All the captains in the many iterations of *Star Trek* have their ups and their downs. I have my personal favorite (obviously *Picard* is the best, right?) and you may have a different opinion of who is the best. But what about the Klingon captains? Nobody ever brings their leadership into the equation. Maybe there's a *Star Trek* fan out there whose favorite leader is *Kruge*, or *Commander Chang*. Maybe it's *Martok* or *Chancellor Gowron*.

Klingons were introduced late into the first season of the original series *Star Trek*. Originally, they were introduced as an analogy to the Cold War-era Russians, but over the decades and with their re-introduction in *Star Trek: The*

Next Generation, the Klingons evolved into deeply developed characters rich with history, culture, politics, traditions, loyalty, and above all, honor.

I love *Deep Space Nine* and *Lower Decks*. My wife loves *The Next Generation* and *Voyager*. Our kids' introduction to *Star Trek* was through *Prodigy*. We watch some form of *Star Trek* almost every night in our home and that is no exaggeration. New and old, *Star Trek* has been our comfort watch over the years and will continue to be. It is comforting, it is hopeful, and it is special. Making this book has been such an honor. Working with the linguist Marc Okrand-creator of the Klingon language-to get all the words and spelling correct was a dream come true. This book is special to me because *Star Trek* is special to me. I hope this book brings you the same joy it has brought me. That would truly be...honorable.

-Joey Spiotto

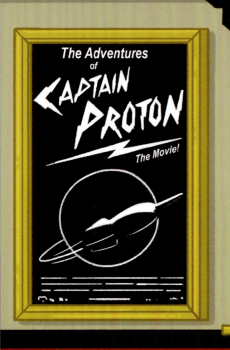

Don't Forget!!! Appt. w/ Dr. Crusher

Buy more warrior's drink.

Maktag

		a good day to die	a good day to die	a good day to die	a good day to die	a good day to die
a good day to die	a good day to die	a good day to die	a good day to die	a good day to die	a good day to die	a good day to die
a good day to die	a good day to die	a good day to die	a good day to die	a good day to die	a good day to die	a good day to die
a good day to die	a good day to die	a good day to die	a good day to die	a good day to die	a good day to die	a good day to die
a good day to die	a good day to die	a good day to die	a good day to die			

Sharpen Bat'leth!

D12-CLASS
BIRD-OF-PREY

0 0 1

DAYS SINCE LAST ACCIDENT

DUE TO: FAULTY PLASMA COILS

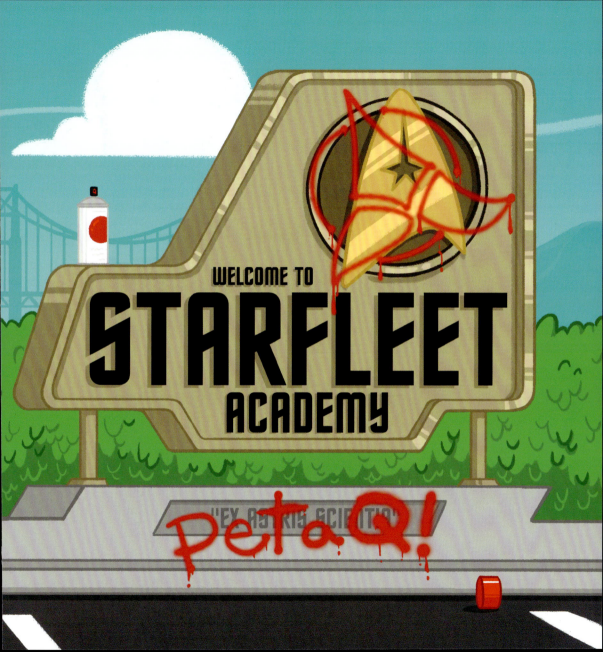

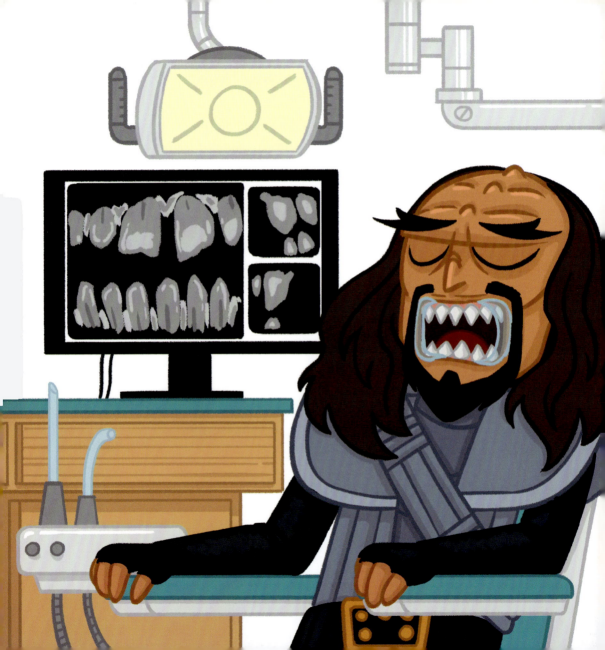

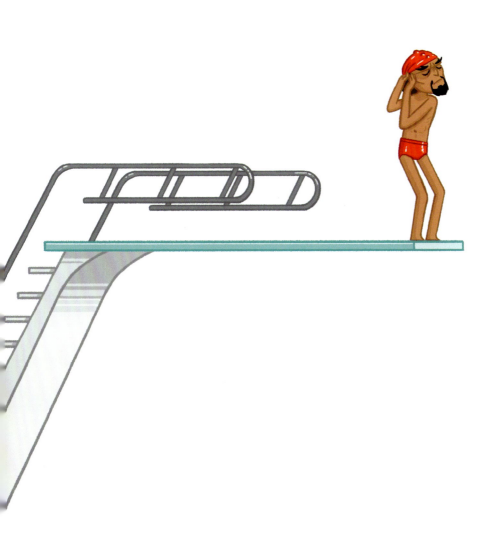

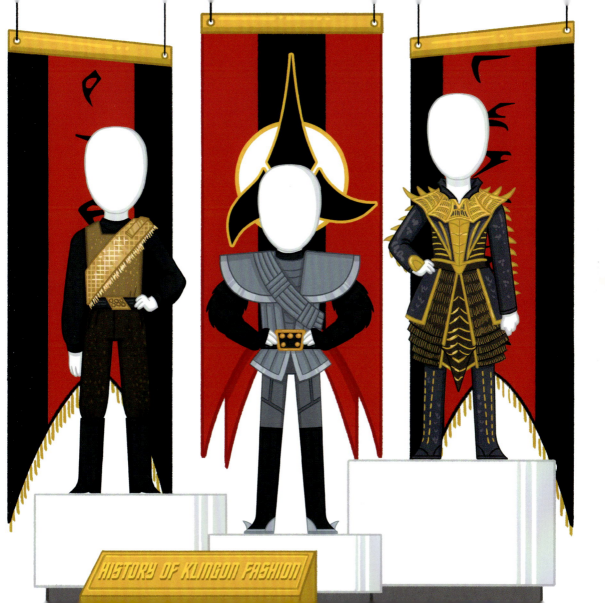

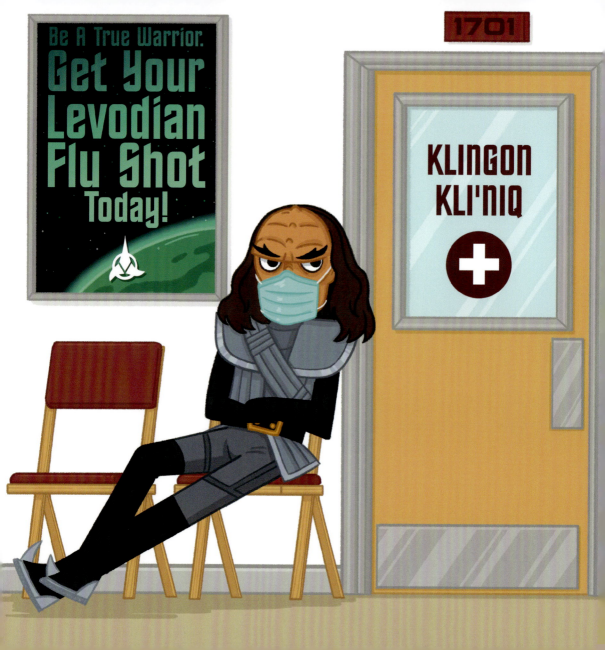

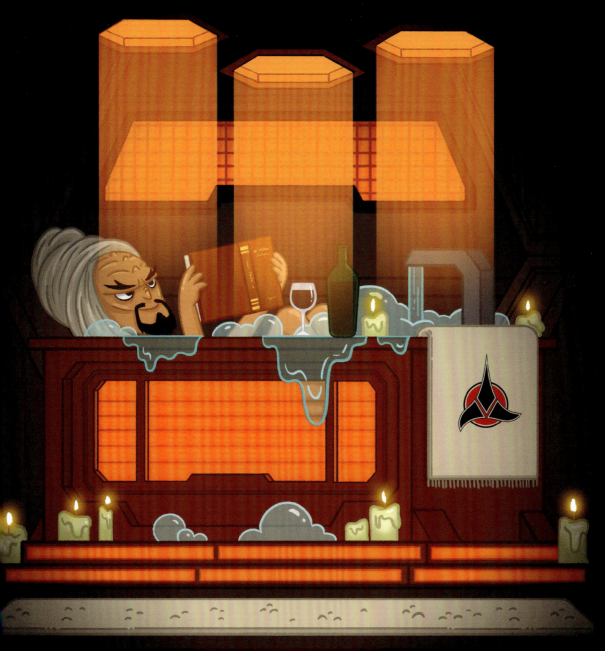

Klingon Glossary

The Klingon language originated when *Star Trek* actor James Doohan and Jon Povill devised a few words for use in *Star Trek: The Motion Picture*. It was then subsequently developed by the American linguist Marc Okrand into a full-fledged language for use in the *Star Trek* films and television series.

Mr. Okrand also graciously consulted on the use of Klingon in this book.

bat'leth-"sword of honor"-a traditional Klingon bladed weapon

cha'DIch-"second" (as in First, second, third...). In legal proceedings where the warrior initiating the proceedings is not allowed to Fight, the warrior appoints a cha'DIch to do the Fighting on his/her behalf

Darsek-the main unit of currency used in the Klingon Empire

Raktajino-Klingon coffee

Qapla'-the Klingon word For "success"

Qo'noS-the Klingon home world

Sword of Kahless-a revered object of the Klingon People and the First bat'leth ever made. It was made by Kahless himself From a lock of his hair dipped into lava

Kahless the Unforgettable-the First Warrior King and Emperor of the Klingon Empire

majQa'-a Klingon phrase of praise, similar to "well done"

petaQ-a Klingon insult that is considered vulgar

par'Mach-the Klingon word For "love"

Sto-vo-kor-a place (like heaven) where the honored dead go

Levodian Flu-a common virus. A modified form of Levodian Flu known as the "Klingon augment virus" threatened to wipe out the Klingon race

The High Council-the ruling body of the Klingon Empire

Bird-of-Prey-a versatile warship utilized by the Klingon Empire

Warp Core-the main energy reactor powering propulsion systems on all warp-capable starships

The Caves of Kahless-caves located on the planet Qo'noS where the Klingon Day of Honor was traditionally observed

Days of the Week

DaSjaj-Monday

Povjaj-Tuesday

ghItlhjaj-Wednesday

loghjaj-Thursday

buqjaj-Friday

ghInjaj-Saturday

jaj wa'-Sunday

K'ISS THE Q'OOK

A note on the apron the Klingon wears on the cover and p37. The apron was made by humans who don't understand the finer points of the Klingon language, and don't realize the words for "kiss" are chop (literally "bite"), or 'ep for human-style kissing. The phrase "Kiss the Cook" would be vutwi' yIchop (for Klingon kissing) or vutwi' yI'ep (for human kissing). But humans are lazy, as we know.

To learn more about the Klingon Language,
visit the Klingon Language Institute at

www.kli.org

About the Author

Joey Spiotto is a *New York Times* bestselling author and illustrator and a graduate of ArtCenter College of Design in beautiful Pasadena, California. He has written and/or illustrated many books, including the hit graphic novel series *Grumpy Unicorn*, the *Little Troublemaker* picture books, the wildly popular *Alien Next Door*, and more.

He has exhibited artwork at multiple pop-culture art galleries and comic book conventions around the world, and designed toys, T-shirts, and collectibles. Before making books, Joey worked in the film and video games industry as a concept artist on notable titles such as *The Polar Express*, *Dead Space*, and *The Sims*.

Joey lives in Southern California with his wife, his two children, and one lovely little cat. You can visit him online at www.joeyspiotto.com